GOOD VIBES *only*

Journal

This journal is dedicated to my mom Ms. Ann Marie Gallaway.

Shortly after she passed away on July 20, 1990, when I was 10 years old, I found her journal. In it were all of her thoughts, her day to day plans and future goals.

She also wrote out her budget and her example is a must for me now.

I spent hours reading all of my mom's entries. She had such beautiful handwriting. Some of them were personal. Other entries made me smile because I felt like I was getting to know my mom better though she wasn't physically here with me.

So, for years now I have been writing in my journal almost daily. I have them for different reasons like free writing my thoughts, for my plans, my budget and so on.

I thank my mom for choosing me to be her daughter and being such an amazing inspiration.

> *Trust the Process...*

> Be Nice...

> *Be Kind...*

> *Be Better...*

> *I create my personal abundance from an infinite source...*

"*Today I focus on what I want to attract in my life...*"

> *From this moment forward I invite unlimited abundance into my life...*

> *Today I embrace my potential to be, do, and have whatever I can dream...*

> *Everything I desire is within me...*

> *I use my conscience intention to manifest my dreams...*

> *Through the law of pure potential, I can create anything anytime anywhere...*

> *Today and every day I give what I want to receive...*

> *Today I made great choices because they are made with full awareness...*

> *I expect and accept abundance to flow easily to me...*

> *As I let go of the need to arrange my life, the universe brings abundant of good to me...*

> *There is a way I can fulfill my true purpose in life...*

> "A good head and a good heart are always a formidable combination." – Nelson Mandela

> "You're never too old to set a new goal or dream a new dream." – C.S Lewis

> "Always be a first rate version of yourself, instead of a second rate version of someone else."
> – Judy Garland.

> *I am successful in whatever I do...*

> *I plan my work and work my plan...*

> *I focus on what is truly essential...*

> *I will make the most of new opportunities...*

> *Good flows to me, good flows from me...*

> *I feel wonderful and alive...*

> *I feel the joy of abundance...*

> *I speak with confidence and calm assurance...*

> *The universe provides for my every want and need...*

> *I am healthy and happy...*

" I have a lot of energy... "

> *I radiate happiness...*

> *I am successful in whatever I do...*

> *Everything is getting better every day...*

> My mind is calm...

> *I am always on the path of success and victory...*

> *I am at peace with myself...*

> *I find peace and joy in all aspects of my life...*

> *I have value and I matter...*

> *I am a success in all that I do...*

> *I am happy...*

> *I feel joy, love, and abundance...*

> *I am one with my inner child...*

I am amazing...

> *I can do anything...*

> *I am prepared to succeed...*

> *Positivity is a choice...*

> *I am fabulous, funny, and giving...*

> *I am outstanding...*

> *I am unique, special, and most importantly, I am me...*

> *I am financially free...*

> *I am perfect exactly as I am...*

> *God loves me...*

> *I make positive healthy choices...*

> *I am in control of my reactions...*

> *I find all solutions within me...*

All is well in my life...

> *I receive blessings and I am a blessing...*

> *I organize my priorities with clarity...*

> *I forgive myself...*

> *I am forgiven...*

> *I will always be there for myself...*

> *I enjoy the variety of life...*

> *I am my own guru...*

> *I take good care of myself...*

> *I am patient with myself...*

> *I let go of my past...*

> *I am evolving eternally...*

> *I know I can always upgrade...*

> *There is a gift for me in everything that I experience...*

> I follow my inner guidance...

> *I appreciate my physical body...*

> *I treat my body well...*

I take it easy...

> *I make room for fun and playfulness...*

> *I appreciate intimacy...*

> *I am very good at letting go...*

> *I am grateful for my life...*

> *I love being myself...*

> *Time is on my side...*

> *I surrender to love...*

> *I invite bliss...*

> *I learn from my past...*

> *I am good at walking the talk...*

> I enjoy being taken good care of by the universe...

> *I create my reality on a continuous basis...*

> *My body is healthy...*

> *I am superior to negative thoughts and low actions...*

> *I forgive those who have harmed me in my past and peacefully detach from them...*

> *I possess the qualities needed to be extremely successful...*

> *My ability to conquer my challenges are limitless...*

My potential to succeed is infinite...

> *I am courageous and I stand up for myself...*

> *My thoughts are filled with positivity and my life is plentiful with prosperity...*

> *I am blessed with an incredible family and wonderful friends...*

> *I am a powerhouse...*

> *My future is an ideal projection of what I envision now...*

> *I radiate beauty, charm, and grace...*

> *I am conquering my illness...*

> *I wake up today with strength in my heart and clarity in my mind...*

> *My fears of tomorrow are simply melting away...*

> *My life is just beginning...*

> *I assert that positive living works...*

> *I always have everything I need to be happy...*

> *I live a positive life and only attract the best...*

> *I am peacefully allowing my life to unfold...*

> *Today, and every day, I choose to be happy...*

> *I am fun energetic and people love me for it...*

> *My life overflows with happiness and love...*

> *Today is rich with opportunity and I open my heart to receive them...*

> *I take the time to show my friends that I care about them...*

> *I am thankful that I get to live another day...*

> *I see the world with beauty and color...*

> *I deserve whatever good comes my way today...*